Easy Salad Recipes

by Debbie Madson

www.kids-cooking-activities.com

© Copyright 2013
All Rights Reserved, Debbie Madson
Images from Bigstockphoto
Many thanks to our Kids-Cooking-Activities readers for contributing their favorite salad recipes for this collaboration cookbook.

About the Author

Debbie Madson is a Web Publisher and Author for children. She has several learning kids websites including:

www.kids-cooking-activities.com
www.kids-sewing-projects.com
www.teaching-kids-money-skills.com

As well as teaching products to aid in these subjects through her websites and TeachersPayTeachers store.
http://www.teacherspayteachers.com/Store/Debbie-Madson

She has many Kindle ebooks for kids fun and entertainment. Debbie also has three kids who are great for helping and contributing to her projects.

All rights Reserved. No part of this publication or the information in it may be quoted from or reproduced in any form by means such as printing, scanning, photocopying or otherwise without prior written permission of the copyright holder.

Disclaimer and Terms of Use: Effort has been made to ensure that the information in this book is accurate and complete, however, the author and the publisher do not warrant the accuracy of the information, text and graphics contained within the book due to the rapidly changing nature of science, research, known and unknown facts and internet. The Author and the publisher do not hold any responsibility for errors, omissions or contrary interpretation of the subject matter herein. This book is presented solely for motivational and informational purposes only.

Contents

Oriental Chicken Salad 6

Wonton Chicken Salad 7

Mandarin Orange Salad 8

Potato Egg Salad 9

Red Potato Salad Recipe 10

Sweet Potato Salad 10

Polish Summer Salad 10

Romaine Fruit Salad 12

Spinach Fruit Salad Recipe 14

Watermelon Salad 14

Fruit and Pudding Salad 16

Peach Strawberry Salad 17

Classic Waldorf Salad 18

Ambrosia Salad 20

Orange Fluff 21

Doritos Taco Salad Recipe 22

Mexican Chicken Taco Salad 22

Simple Taco Salad 23

Taco Salad with Chili 23

Chicken Nacho Salad 25

Cobb Salad 27

Grilled Chopped Salad with Prawns 28

Turkey and Avocado Salad 30

Fruity Carrot Salad 31

Vegetable Shredded Salad 31

Hawaiian Carrot Salad 33

Chicken Pasta Salad 34

Fruit Chicken Salad 36

Milena's Quick an' Simple Chicken Salad Recipe 37

Spicy and Zesty Chicken Salad in a Bell Pepper Cup 38

Tortellini Pasta Salad 40

BLT Pasta Salad Recipe 41

Pesto Salad 42

7 Layer Salad 43

Mini Layered Salads 44

Pasta Salad 45

Mediterranean Grilled Zucchini Pasta Salad 46

Italian Pepper Pasta 47

Greek Salad 49

Ham and Orzo salad recipe 50

Green Bean Salad recipe 51

Broccoli Salad 52

Three Bean Salad 53

Pepperoni Caesar Salad 54

Quick Caprese on the go 55

Avocado Delight 56

Grilled Lime Chicken Salad 57

Top Ramen Salad 58

Avocado, Tomato, Mozzarella Salad 59

Asian Rice Salad 60

Beef and Pasta Salad 61

Creamy Stuffed Pears 62

Egg Macaroni Salad 63

Ravioli Spring Salad 64

Cool Cottage Cheese Salad 65

Cucumber Chicken Salad 66

Italian Floret Salad 67

Apple Banana Peanut Butter Salad 68

Classic Chicken Curry And Green Grape Salad 69

Easy Spaghetti Caprese 70

Ranch Style Peas And Carrots Pasta Salad 71

Mozzarella Two Bean Salad 72

Bow Tie Melon Salad 73

Refreshing Cucumber Salad Bowls 74

Fruit Salad with Zest 76

Make Ahead Veggie Pasta Salad 77

Steak Salad with Asian Chili Sauce 78

Potato and Pea Salad 80

Almond Cranberry Pasta Salad 81

Sweet Red Apple Slaw 82

Oriental Chicken Salad

Medium iceberg lettuce
2 Cups cooked, cubed or shredded chicken
1 Cup cashews
8 oz. water chestnuts
1 Cup green peas
3 oz. can chow mein noodles
Mix together, pour dressing over salad and toss to coat. Serve immediately.

Dressing:
½ Cup sugar
1 Tablespoon cornstarch
¼ Cup water
¼ Cup vegetable oil
¼ Cup ketchup
3 Tablespoons cider vinegar
1 Tablespoon soy sauce
Combine in saucepan and bring to a boil, cook and stir 2 minutes.

Wonton Chicken Salad

6 chicken breasts, cooked and shredded
1/2-1 head lettuce, washed and torn
3 cups fresh spinach washed
3/4 Cup swiss cheese, shredded
1 cup cottage cheese
1 pkg. wonton wrappers cut in half and fried

Dressing:
3/4 Cup white vinegar
1 1/2 cup oil
3/4 cup sugar
1 1/2 teaspoon grated onion
1 1/2 teaspoon salt
3/4 teaspoon dry mustard
Assemble salad but only add wontons just before serving.
Toss with dressing. Serves 10-12.

Mandarin Orange Salad

1/2 cup almonds, slivered sautéed with 3 tablespoons sugar
Romaine lettuce, spinach and iceberg lettuce use a combination of each or whichever you like
1/2 red onion, sweet, sliced into rings
1 Cup green peas or pea pods
small can mandarin orange segments, drained

Dressing:
3 tablespoons orange juice
3 tablespoons olive oil
2 tablespoons cider vinegar
1 tablespoon honey
pinch of salt

Mix dressing ingredients in a jar or measuring cup. Chill until ready to serve. To prep salad, toss greens in a serving bowl, add onion, oranges and almonds. Serve with dressing but don't pour dressing on until ready to serve.

Potato Egg Salad

4 medium potatoes, diced and cooked
2 boiled eggs, chopped
 *optional ingredients could be chopped onion or chopped celery

Dressing:

1/2 Cup mayonnaise
1/2 Cup miracle whip
2 Tablespoons vinegar
1 teaspoon salt
1 teaspoon sugar
1/4 teaspoon pepper

In serving bowl add potatoes and eggs. Set aside. Add all dressing ingredients together and blend well. Stir dressing into potato egg salad and chill for several hours before serving. You can also sprinkle the top with paprika.

Red Potato Salad Recipe

2 lbs. red potatoes, diced and cooked
2 boiled eggs, chopped
Dressing:
1/2 Cup plain yogurt
1/4 Cup sour cream
Add diced, cooked potatoes and chopped eggs together in serving bowl. Blend yogurt and sour cream together and mix into potato salad.

Sweet Potato Salad

3 sweet potatoes, diced and cooked
1 egg, hard-boiled and sliced
1/4 cup green onions, chopped
Dressing:
1/4 cup sugar
1/4 cup vinegar
Add potatoes, onions and egg in serving bowl. Mix sugar and vinegar together and drizzle over sweet potato salad. Chill.

Polish Summer Salad

2 medium cooked white potatoes
7-8 cooked carrots
1/8 of a leek
8 -10 hardboiled eggs
1 jar of refrigerated, kosher dill pickles
1 can of sweet peas or cooked garden fresh peas

Dice potatoes, carrots, leek, eggs, and pickles. Drain peas and add to the other vegetables. Mix with mayonnaise to the desired consistency.

Romaine Fruit Salad
romaine lettuce cut up
avocado cut in slices
kiwi cut up
assorted fruit such as watermelon, grapes, blueberries, grapefruit, strawberries, orange segments
Toss ingredients together and serve with one of the dressings below.

Citrus Salad Dressing Recipe
1/3 Cup oil
1 teaspoon orange peel
½ Cup grapefruit juice
2 Tablespoons sugar
2 Tablespoons lemon juice
½ teaspoon mustard
¼ teaspoon salt
Mix ingredients together and pour over salad. Store in the fridge for up to two weeks.

Honey dressing
4 teaspoons lime juice
2 teaspoons honey
¼ teaspoons salt
3 Tablespoons vegetable oil
Mix ingredients together and pour over salad. Store in the fridge for up to two weeks.

Spinach Fruit Salad Recipe

fresh spinach or romaine lettuce
fruit of choice: sliced strawberries, sliced kiwi, grapefruit sections, watermelon balls etc. Add spinach and chopped fruit to serving bowl. Pour dressing on right before serving.
Dressing:
1 C. oil
4 T. sour cream
5 T. vinegar
½ tsp. mustard
2 garlic cloves
½ tsp. salt
2 T. sugar
2 tsp. parsley
Blend oil and sour cream. Then mix in vinegar and other ingredients. Shake well before using.

Watermelon Salad

1 Cup seeded chopped watermelon
1/2 Cup chopped strawberries
½ Cup chopped kiwifruit
½ Cup chopped peaches
3 Tablespoons lime juice
4 teaspoons honey
1-2 mint leaves, chopped, optional
Mix all ingredients together. Serve in halved and hollowed limes for added affect, in hollowed out watermelon, or inside half a coconut, hollowed pineapple, etc.

Fruit and Pudding Salad
2 cups peaches, sliced
2 cups strawberries
2 cups grapes
2 cups bananas sliced
1 1/4 cups milk
1/2 cup sour cream or plain yogurt
1 package vanilla or banana pudding
6 ounce can crushed pineapple with juice
In a bowl, combine milk, sour cream and pudding mixture. Gently stir in pineapple. Chill. In a serving bowl, layer peaches, strawberries, grapes and bananas. You can add a different fruit, use whatever you like. Pour pudding mixture over the top and let chill several hours before serving.

Peach Strawberry Salad

1 Cup strawberries

1 Cup plain or vanilla yogurt

1 Cup peaches

1-2 Tablespoons sugar

dash cinnamon

In a serving bowl add strawberries and peaches. In a separate bowl, stir together yogurt, sugar and cinnamon. Pour over top of fruit. Gently fold into mixture to cover.

Classic Waldorf Salad

This salad dates back to the late 1800's where the New York Waldorf-Astoria hotel served this. It originally only had mayonnaise, apples and celery. We've added a few more ingredients.

4 Cups shredded Romaine lettuce, optional
2 red apples, diced
1 Tablespoon lemon juice
¼ Cup grapes, halved
½ Cup walnuts, chopped
2 stalks celery, sliced
½ Cup mayonnaise
1/4 Cup sour cream
juice of 1 lemon

In a mixing bowl add apples, grapes, walnuts and celery. Blend together mayonnaise, sour cream and lemon juice in different bowl. Add sour cream mixture to fruit salad and stir to coat. In a serving bowl, lay lettuce on bottom of bowl. Spoon fruit salad on top of lettuce. Chill before serving.

Ambrosia Salad
bag mini marshmallows
18 oz. can mandarin oranges
large can crushed pineapple -drained
small jar maraschino cherries, cut in half
1 can peaches, diced
1 Cup shredded coconut
32 oz. flavored yogurt, plain yogurt or sour cream
In a serving bowl, add marshmallows, oranges, pineapple, peaches, cherries and coconut. Stir yogurt into fruit mixture and stir until well combined.

A **frog eye salad** is much similar to this recipe but has cooked acini di pepe pasta stirred into the recipe. Acini di pepe are small round pasta that resemble frog eyes!

Orange Fluff
by Flora (USA)

1 small box orange Jell-O
1-16 oz small curd cottage cheese
1 can mandarin oranges, drained and diced
small 1 can crushed pineapple, drained
1 large cool whip

1) In a large bowl combine cottage cheese and orange jello, fold together.
2) After draining all fruit and dicing oranges, add these to cheese mix in bowl. Mix well.
3) Fold in cool whip gently, be sure to mix well.
4) Place this in refrigerator for at least 1 hr to set well.

Doritos Taco Salad Recipe

Doritos chips

Ground hamburger, cooked

Taco salad ingredients such as lettuce, tomatoes, cheese, onions, olives, etc

Salad Dressing whichever you'd like I like Ranch others like a tomato based dressing

Add shredded lettuce to your serving bowl. Add in other salad ingredients and cooked hamburger. Toss together. Crush chips and add to salad. Serve immediately and top with dressing of choice.

Mexican Chicken Taco Salad

1 avocado, chopped and sprinkled with lemon juice

1 16-ounce can kidney or black beans or mixture of both

2 cups lettuce shredded

2 tomatoes, chopped

Can corn, drained

2 cups chicken shredded cooked

4 ounces sharp cheddar cheese shredded (about 1 cup)

Mix all ingredients together and toss. Serve with sour cream, salsa or ranch dressing.

Simple Taco Salad

Ground hamburger
Taco seasoning
Kidney beans
Shredded cheddar cheese
Shredded lettuce
Chopped tomatoes
Sliced olives
Cook hamburger and season with taco seasoning and pepper. Have kids shred lettuce and mix salad ingredients together.
~Another way you can serve this is in individual bowls and everyone in the family can build their own taco salad.

Taco Salad with Chili

Find a recipe for chili or use your favorite. Drain most the liquid off your chili. This will give you a thicker chili.

Shred lettuce and have the following toppings available for family to pick from.
Shredded cheese
Sliced olives
Sour cream
Diced onions
Tortilla chips
Serve in a large bowl with lettuce on the bottom, chili on top and sprinkle with desired toppings.

Chicken Nacho Salad

by Morgan (USA)

I have lots of fun making these with my mom.

Serves 4 people

Ingredients:

For Salad:

4 precooked frozen breaded chicken strips

1 bag Romaine Lettuce

1/2 cup crushed Cool Ranch Doritos

1/2 cup Colby cheese, shredded

For Dressing:

3/4 cup Salsa

3/4 cup Ranch Dressing

Directions:

1. Reheat the chicken as directed.

2. In a small bowl, mix the ranch dressing and salsa together.

3. Slice the cooked chicken into bite-sized pieces.

4. Thoroughly toss together the lettuce, chicken, cheese and dressing in a large salad bowl.

Cobb Salad

Romaine lettuce
Fresh baby spinach
Shredded cheddar cheese or other type
Chicken breasts, cooked and sliced
diced ham
diced turkey
cooked bacon
2 hard boiled eggs, sliced in quarters
avocado, cut in slices
tomatoes cut in quarters

In a serving bowl, add lettuce and spinach to bottom. Sprinkle with cheese and arrange remaining ingredients attractively in your bowl.

Grilled Chopped Salad with Prawns
by Tamar (USA)

2 heads Grilled Romaine Lettuce
1 ear Corn (husk and silk removed)
1 zucchini halved lengthwise
12 jumbo shrimp/prawns (peeled and deveined)
2 red peppers
dash garlic powder
2 ripe avocados (peeled and diced into 1/2 inch pieces)
1 bunch chopped cilantro
1 cup peeled & diced jicama
2 cups tortilla strips
1/2 cup roasted pepitas (out of shell)
1/2 cup crumbled feta cheese

Dressing:
3 tablespoons olive oil
2 tablespoons fresh lemon juice
1 tablespoon fresh lime juice
1 tablespoons agave or honey
sea salt and fresh ground pepper to taste

Lightly coat both heads of romaine, corn, zucchini, red peppers, and shrimp with olive oil, dust with garlic powder, and grill until done. Chop/dice the vegetables into 1/2" pieces.

Prepare the dressing by blending ingredients together thoroughly.
Set aside the shrimp and cheese.
In a large bowl, mix together the chopped grilled vegetables with the remaining ingredients and the dressing.

Divide the salad onto 4 plates, and top each salad with 3 jumbo shrimp. Sprinkle cheese on the tops of the salads.

Turkey and Avocado Salad

2 cups of cooked and sliced turkey
1 large avocado sliced
2 red apples, cored and sliced
Bunch of mixed salad leaves
2 apples, cored and cut in chunks
1/2 Cup pecans, chopped
4 oz. blue cheese, crumbled

Dressing:

3 tablespoons apple juice
3 tablespoons natural unflavored yogurt
1 teaspoon honey
1 teaspoon mustard
2 oz of toasted pine nuts for garnish

Place all the salad items in a large bowl and gently toss together. In a separate bowl mix all the dressing ingredients together except the pine nuts. Pour dressing over the salad and top with toasted pine nuts. To toast the pine nuts place a little olive oil or non stick spray in a non stick frying pan and toast the pine nuts for approximately 2 minutes.

Fruity Carrot Salad

2 Cups shredded carrots
1/4 Cup coconut
handful of craisins
Add carrots, coconut and craisins together in serving bowl. Drizzle with honey and toss to coat.

Vegetable Shredded Salad

shredded carrots
shredded zucchini
chopped nuts
Add ingredients to serving bowl. Drizzle with olive oil and salt and pepper.

Other ideas for a basic carrot salad

- Add Craisins in place of raisins.
- Add a sprinkle of ginger.
- Add 1/2-1 teaspoon sugar or honey.
- Add chopped pineapple.
- Add shredded coconut.
- Boil carrots in orange juice for more flavor and more tender carrots.
- Serve warm or cold.
- Add a dash of hot sauce.
- Use olive oil and lemon juice in place of mayo and yogurt.

Hawaiian Carrot Salad

4 Cups shredded carrots
large can pineapple tidbits in juice, drain and save juice*
1/2 cup raisins
1/2 cup shredded coconut
1 cup mayonnaise
1 cup almonds, cashews or peanuts (add right before serving)

Place shredded carrots, pineapple, raisins and coconut in serving bowl. In a glass or measuring cup stir together mayonnaise and pineapple juice*. Pour over carrot salad and chill. Before serving add nuts.

Chicken Pasta Salad

3 cups chicken cooked and shredded or cubed
2 cups chopped celery
1 cup slivered or chopped almonds
4 hard boiled eggs
1 cup chopped pickles
1 Tablespoon lemon juice
1/4 teaspoon salt
1 1/4 Cup mayonnaise
1 Cup shredded cheddar cheese

In mixing bowl, add cooked chicken, celery, cheese, almonds, chopped eggs, and pickles. Stir ingredients together. In separate bowl, add mayonnaise, salt, and lemon juice together. Mix into chicken mixture. Spread on croissant, hard roll or pita bread.

This recipe can be made ahead of time. It can also be served warmed up in the oven. Kids can help by adding ingredients and chopping hard boiled eggs with a table knife.

Fruit Chicken Salad

4-5 chicken breasts cubed or shredded chicken
1 tbsp + 1 tsp dry Caribbean jerk seasoning, divided
1 tsp lime zest, grated
1/4 C lime juice
1 tbsp honey
1 (8 oz.) can pineapple chunks, drained
8 Cups of mixed salad greens
1/2 cantaloupe, diced

Mix together seasoning, lime zest, lime juice and honey. Pour into sealable ziploc bag or container and marinate chicken several hours. Cook chicken and pour off excess marinade. In a serving bowl, mix chicken, pineapple, salad and cantaloupe.

Milena's Quick an' Simple Chicken Salad Recipe
by Milena (Johannesburg)

2 cooked chicken breasts skinned and cut into thin strips.
1 bunch of baby spinach leaves torn into pieces.
225g (or just 2 potatoes per person) small potatoes cooked.
1 cup mayonnaise
1 cup sour cream
salt (to taste)
freshly ground pepper (to taste)
half a cup cashew nuts (optional)
Mix the chicken with the potatoes, spinach leaves, and cashew nuts.
Blend the sour cream with mayonnaise, salt, and pepper. Mix the sauce in with the chicken mixture. Sprinkle a little bit of cashew nuts on top to decorate. Spoon into a salad bowl and pop into fridge to chill.

Spicy and Zesty Chicken Salad in a Bell Pepper Cup
by Jane (PA)

Ingredients:

2 Skinless Boneless Chicken Breast Cubed
3 Jalapeno Pepper(Pickled and Finely Chopped)
1 Leave worth of Chopped Lettuce
3 Tablespoons Ranch Dressing
1/4 cup Mayonnaise
1 Teaspoon Dried Parsley Flakes
Salt 'n' Pepper
4 Red Bell Peppers

Directions:

1. Sear Chicken on both sides in a skillet until fully cooked. Then lay aside.
2. Cut Tops off of Bell Peppers. Take seeds out and place on lightly greased baking sheet and roast for approximately 5 minutes.
3. Cube up chicken and take peppers out of the oven.
4. Combine jalapenos, chicken, lettuce, ranch dressing, mayo, parsley, salt 'n' pepper in a bowl until completely blended.
5. Stuff peppers with chicken salad.

Tortellini Pasta Salad

8 oz. frozen tortellini, cooked and cooled
1 cucumber, diced
1 tomato, diced
1/3 Cup feta cheese
1/3 Cup black olives, sliced
1/4 Cup chopped nuts
Olive oil
Salt and pepper

Cook tortellini and allow to cool about 10 minutes. In salad bowl, add cucumber, tomato, crumbled feta cheese and black olives. Drizzle olive oil over salad and toss. Sprinkle with salt and pepper. Sprinkle nuts over top.

BLT Pasta Salad Recipe

6 oz. elbow macaroni, cooked
8 slices bacon cooked, cut up
1 large Tomato cut up
4 Cups lettuce cut up

Dressing:

1 Cup mayo or salad dressing
1/4 Cup lemon juice from concentrate
2 teaspoons chicken bouillon
2 teaspoons sugar

In a salad bowl, add cooked macaroni and tomato. Stir together dressing ingredients and blend together. Pour over macaroni and chill in fridge. Before serving stir in lettuce and chopped bacon and serve immediately.

Pesto Salad

pasta

chopped tomatoes

pesto

Cook pasta and drain. Toss with pesto and chopped tomatoes. You can add more chopped vegetables that you like, too.

7 Layer Salad

1 Cup noodles, cooked
3 Cups shredded lettuce
3-4 hard cooked eggs, sliced
salt and pepper
1 Cup chopped cooked ham
1 Cup chopped salami
1 pkg. Frozen peas, thawed
½ Cup mayonnaise
¼ Cup sour cream
1 teaspoon mustard
1 Cup cheese

Cook macaroni and rinse with cold water.

In serving bowl , (I like to use a glass bowl so you can see the layers) place lettuce on bottom, top with cooked noodles, cooked chopped eggs, chopped ham, salami and peas.Combine mayo, sour cream and mustard together and spread over the top. Refrigerate overnight.

Sprinkle with cheese before serving.

Mini Layered Salads

Lettuce

Cooked noodles

Boiled eggs

chopped carrots

Fresh or frozen peas, unthawed

Salad dressing of choice

Cook 1-2 cups of noodles until tender. In a separate pan boil eggs, about one per person. Allow to cool. In a glass cup or clear plastic cups (so you can see the layers), layer lettuce, noodles, eggs, carrots, peas and drizzle with salad dressing.

Pasta Salad
by Tot Snob Kelly
Any kind of Pasta
Deli Turkey cut up small
Frozen Peas (defrosted in hot water)
Cherry Tomatoes cut in half
Toss with olive oil and salt

Mediterranean Grilled Zucchini Pasta Salad

by Faiza (Pakistan)

2 cups diced prepared smoked chicken sausage
300 grams of prepared frozen cheese filled tortellini
2 medium sized diced red bell pepper
2 medium sized sliced zucchini
2 cups diced cottage cheese
1/2 cup oil-packed sun-dried tomato
1/2 teaspoon garlic powder

For the dressing:

1/2 teaspoon dried oregano
2 tablespoons lemon juice
1/2 cup olive oil
3 tablespoons white vinegar (optional)
1 finely chopped garlic clove

Cook tortellini pasta according to the directions on the package. Grease the grill pan with cooking oil. Toss zucchini slices with garlic powder and grill on the greased grill pan on medium-low heat for about 3-4 minutes per side. Squeeze out the excess oil from the sun-dried tomatoes.

To prepare the dressing, whisk white vinegar with olive oil, oregano, lemon juice and garlic powder in a mixing bowl. In large bowl, toss grilled cooked pasta, sun-dried tomatoes and zucchini along with all the other ingredients with the prepared dressing and serve.

Italian Pepper Pasta

8 oz. of uncooked bow tie pasta
12 oz. Italian sausage links, cut into 1 in pieces
2 red sweet peppers cut into pieces
1/2 Cup of beef broth
1/4 tsp pepper

Cook the pasta as directed on the package and drain well.
Place the sausage and peppers into a large skillet.
Cook the mixture over medium high heat for 5 minutes, stirring often, or until the sausage is browned and the peppers are tender.
Drain off any fat.
Pour the broth into the skillet.
Stir in the pepper and bring the mixture to a boil.
Reduce the heat to low and cook 5 minutes.
Pour the mixture over the pasta and stir to coat the pasta completely.

Makes 4 servings

Greek Salad

3 tomatoes, diced
2 cucumbers, peeled and diced
1 red or yellow pepper, diced
1 small red onion, diced
1 cup crumbled feta cheese
black Greek olives, pitted and sliced
1/4 cup olive oil
4 teaspoons lemon juice
1 1/2 teaspoons dried oregano
salt and pepper to taste

Add tomatoes, cucumbers, pepper, and onion in a serving bowl. Gently add in feta cheese and olives. In a small bowl or cup blend together olive oil, lemon juice, oregano, and season with salt and pepper. Drizzle over salad and serve.

Ham and Orzo salad recipe

½ Cup orzo, tiny tube macaroni or tiny star pasta
1 Cup frozen mixed peas, corn and carrots
8 oz. ham, cubed

Dressing

½ Cup plain yogurt
1 cucumber chopped fine
1/4 tsp. mixed herbs or dill weed

Boil water and cook pasta add peas and carrots last few minutes. Drain and rinse with cold water when tender. Stir together pasta peas and carrots and ham. In small bowl mix dressing. Pour over salad mix and chill 4 hours.
Add chopped romaine lettuce if desired.

Green Bean Salad recipe
fresh whole green beans
blue cheese or feta cheese
chopped nuts such as almonds or pecans
cooked and chopped bacon
Boil green beans until tender and drain. Place in serving bowl toss with cheese, nuts and bacon.

Broccoli Salad
large bunch broccoli
3 stalks celery, chopped
bacon fried crisp and diced
1 Cup sunflower seeds or almonds
Swiss cheese, grated
1 onion, sliced in rings
1 Cup raisins, optional

Dressing:
1 Cup mayonnaise
2 Tablespoons vinegar
¼ Cup sugar

In a serving bowl, add washed and chopped broccoli. Add in celery, bacon, seeds, onion, swiss cheese and raisins. Toss salad ingredients together. In a measuring cup stir together mayonnaise, vinegar and sugar. Drizzle over salad and serve.

Three Bean Salad

1 can green beans
1 can wax beans, drained
1 can dark red kidney beans, drained
Dressing:
1/4 cup vegetable oil
1/4 cup cider vinegar
1/2 cup sugar
pinch of salt and pepper

In serving bowl, blend three beans together. In measuring cup, stir together vegetable oil, cider vinegar, sugar and season with salt and pepper. Pour over bean salad and chill several hours.

Pepperoni Caesar Salad

Salad:
Romaine lettuce torn up
1 C. halved thinly sliced pepperoni
1 ½ C. Caesar salad croutons
¼ C. shredded parmesan cheese

Dressing:
1/3 C olive oil
2 T. cider vinegar
2 T. mayonnaise
2 T. garlic cloves, minced
½ tsp. mustard
¼ tsp. Worcestershire sauce
1/4 tsp. pepper

Combine salad and dressing. Serve immediately.

Quick Caprese on the go
by Cameron (USA)

half a roma tomato chopped
1-2 tbsp finely shredded basil leaves
half cup cottage cheese
1-2 tbsp extra-virgin olive oil
salt and pepper

Mix the tomato, basil, and cottage cheese together in a leak-proof to-go container, drizzle with olive oil and sprinkle with salt and pepper to taste. I like this snack because I do karate, and it is light, refreshing, and healthy to eat. I take it with me when I am training at the dojo.

Avocado Delight
by Annalena Marie (USA)

3 avocados, chopped
1 bag of salad mix
2 tomatoes, chopped
Chopped almonds
Corn chips, broken into pieces

1. Mix all the food together well with your hands. (Make sure they're clean.)
2. Pour into a medium size bowl
3. Mix again
4. Gently put the salad on plates
5. Make sure it looks like a fancy restaurant would
6. Enjoy!

Grilled Lime Chicken Salad

1 lb. boneless chicken cut in strips
1/3 cup olive oil
2 limes juiced
1/4 cup white wine vinegar
1 teaspoon yellow mustard
1 clove garlic, minced
1/2 teaspoon seasoning salt
1/4 teaspoon pepper

In a ziploc bag add oil, limes, vinegar, mustard, garlic, salt and pepper. Add in chicken and seal shut. Marinate in fridge several hours. Grill.
To make into a salad add:
grilled chicken, cut in pieces
black beans
corn
shredded lettuce
shredded cheese

Top Ramen Salad

1 Cabbage cut up
1 pkg. Chicken flavor Ramen noodles crunched up
slivered almonds
sunflower seeds
3-4 carrots shredded
Toss together. Pour dressing over top. Serve immediately.

Dressing:
3 T white vinegar
3 T. white sugar
½ C. oil
seasoning from top ramen noodles
1/8 tsp. Salt
1/8 tsp. pepper

Avocado, Tomato, Mozzarella Salad

2 avocados cubed
2 tomatoes chopped
mozzarella cheese, cubed
2 tsp. basil
Romaine lettuce
Toss together.

Asian Rice Salad

box Rice a Roni cooked and cooled
20oz. pineapple chunks, drained
chicken cooked and cut up
8 oz. almond slivers
8 oz. water chestnuts, drained and sliced
1 C. golden raisins
2 C red grapes
2 C. celery, sliced
½ red onion, sliced thinly

Dressing:
1T. soy sauce
2 T. lemon juice
1 ½C. mayo
2 tsp curry powder

Combine salad together and pour dressing over top. Stir in onion before serving. Chill overnight.

Beef and Pasta Salad

3 C. pasta cooked and drained
2 tsp. beef flavor bouillon
1 C Italian salad dressing
1 C. cherry tomatoes, halved
1 lb. Beef strips
2 T. vegetable oil
6 oz. provolone cheese, cubed
½ C. sliced olives

Brown meat in 1 tsp. bouillon in oil. Combine meat, pasta, salad dressing and remaining 1 tsp. bouillon. Let stand 15 min. Add remaining ingredients and mix well. Cover and chill. Serve with grated Parmesan cheese

Creamy Stuffed Pears

1 (3 oz) pkg. cream cheese, softened
3 tsp apricot preserves
1 (8 oz) can pineapple tidbits, drained
1 fresh peach or pear, pitted and halved
1 T pecans or any nuts, chopped

Place the cream cheese into a mixing bowl. Add the apricot preserves and with an electric mixer on low speed beat until mixture becomes creamy. Fold in the pineapple tidbits.
Slice a small portion off of the bottom of the pear and peach halves so they will lie on the plate.
Spoon the pineapple mixture onto each of the fruit halves. Sprinkle the top with the pecans for garnish.

Egg Macaroni Salad

2 cups uncooked macaroni or any shaped pasta
2 hard-boiled eggs, chopped fine
2 Tbsp chopped crispy dill pickles
1 stalk celery, chopped fine
1 green onion, chopped fine
3/4 cup Italian dressing

Bring a big pot of salted water to a boil, then add macaroni and cook until al dente; drain well through a colander. In a large bowl, put the macaroni, eggs, pickles, celery, onions, and Italian dressing; toss gently to coat well. Taste and add salt and pepper if desired. Cover bowl and refrigerate for 30 minutes before serving, then serve cold. Serves 2 to 4.

Ravioli Spring Salad

1 lb. ricotta-stuffed fresh ravioli or any type of pasta
1 lb. fresh asparagus, trimmed and cut into 1 inch pieces
2 cups frozen sweet green peas
5 cups fresh baby spinach, washed and dried thoroughly
1/2 cup slivered almonds
2 Tbsp olive oil
1/2 cup Parmesan cheese, freshly shredded

Fill a large pot with water, add 1 teaspoon salt, bring to a boil, and add pasta and cook according to directions.
In the final 1 minute before pasta is done cooking, add the asparagus and peas and continue cooking for 1 minute.
Pour the pasta and vegetables into a large colander and allow to drain thoroughly.
Put cooked pasta and vegetables into a large bowl, and add the spinach, pine nuts, and olive oil - toss to combine well. Taste for flavor and add salt and pepper if desired, then top with Parmesan cheese and serve.

Cool Cottage Cheese Salad

1 1/4 Cup of cottage cheese
1 stalk celery, chopped fine
2 tbsp raisins, optional
2 pear halves, coarsely chopped
1/2 tsp cinnamon

Place the cottage cheese into a bowl. Stir in the celery and raisins well. Fold in the pears.
Sprinkle with the cinnamon and stir well.

Makes 4 servings

Cucumber Chicken Salad

2 Cups cooked chicken, shredded
2 Cups seedless red grapes, halved
1 Cup cucumber, chopped
3 Tablespoons mayonnaise
4 Cups lettuce, shredded

Place the chicken into a large bowl. Add the grapes and cucumbers and toss to combine.
Pour the mayonnaise over the chicken and stir to coat.
Divide the lettuce between four plates.
Top the lettuce with the chicken salad.

Italian Floret Salad

1 head of cauliflower, cut into florets
1 bunch of broccoli, cut into florets
2 Cups or small carton cherry tomatoes
1 (6 oz.) can small ripe olives, pitted and drained
1 Cup Italian salad dressing
1 Cup feta cheese, crumbled

Place the cauliflower and broccoli together in a large serving bowl. Gently fold in the tomatoes and olives. Pour salad dressing over the vegetables tossing to coat. Cover and refrigerate at least 4 hours. Before serving toss again then sprinkle the top with the cheese.

Makes 12 servings

The longer this salad stays covered in the refrigerator the better it will taste. Cooling it helps the Italian flavors to blend into the vegetables.

Apple Banana Peanut Butter Salad

2 red apples, cored and cut into bit size pieces
4 firm bananas, halved and sliced
1/2 Cup cashews or other nuts, chopped
1/2 Cup of mayonnaise,
4 tbsp creamy peanut butter

Place the apples and bananas into a large serving bowl. Add the chopped cashews tossing gently to combine. Place the mayonnaise into a small mixing bowl. Whisk the peanut butter into the mayonnaise until smooth. Pour the mixture over the fruit and stir gently to coat.

Makes 8 servings

Classic Chicken Curry And Green Grape Salad

1 tablespoon lemon juice
6 tablespoon mayonnaise
1 1/2 teaspoon curry powder
1 1/4 teaspoon salt
1/4 teaspoon ground black pepper
3 cups cooked chicken, diced
1 1/2 cup celery, sliced thin
1 cup green seedless grapes
3 tablespoon slivered almonds, toasted
lettuce of your choice

In a large salad bowl, whisk together the lemon juice, mayonnaise, curry powder, salt, and pepper.
Add the bowl the chicken, celery, and grapes, and toss to coat well.
Cover bowl and chill before serving.
To serve, place lettuce on salad plates, spoon chicken salad over, then garnish with slivered almonds.

Easy Spaghetti Caprese

1 pkg (8 oz) uncooked thin spaghetti
1 Tbsp extra-virgin olive oil, more or less as desired
4 large Roma tomatoes, washed and diced
1/4 cup fresh basil leaves, cut chiffonade style
3 ounces fresh soft mozzarella (deli packaged), cut in bite size pieces
8 whole pitted black olives, rough chopped
2 green onions, chopped
salt and pepper to taste

Cook spaghetti in a large pot of boiling water with salt, according to package directions, making sure it remains al dente; drain and put in a very large bowl, add olive oil and toss to coat well, adding a bit more if you want your pasta oilier.
Add the remaining ingredients and toss gently. Taste and add salt and pepper as needed for flavor. Serve at room temperature either on plates or in pasta bowls.
Serves 4.

Ranch Style Peas And Carrots Pasta Salad

1/2 cup mayonnaise
1/2 cup sour cream
1 pkg (1 oz) dry Ranch Style dressing mix
1/2 tsp onion powder
3 cups uncooked shell shaped pasta
1 regular carrot, peeled and shredded (like cheese)
1 cup frozen peas, thawed
1/4 cup crumbled, crisp bacon

In a large bowl, prepare dressing by whisking together the mayonnaise, sour cream, dry dressing mix, and onion powder. Cover bowl and refrigerate for 30 minutes.
Meanwhile prepare the pasta. Bring a pot of salted water to boil, add pasta, and cook just until al dente; drain in colander and set in refrigerator to cool.
Grate the carrots into strips using the large cutter size on a box grater to form strips of carrot.
Let peas thaw at room temperature, or rinse under cold water and drain.
Make sure your bacon is cooked crisp, cooled, and crumbled.
When dressing has cooled for 30 minutes, remove from refrigerator and add pasta to the dressing bowl, then add carrots and peas, and toss to combine.
Cover again and put salad back in the refrigerator for about 1 hour so the flavors can combine.
Remove from refrigerator and sprinkle crumbled bacon over the salad before serving.
Serve chilled.
Will serve 2 to 4 people.

Mozzarella Two Bean Salad

1 (15 oz.) can garbanzo beans, rinsed and drained well
1 (15 oz.) can butter beans, rinsed and drained well
1 cucumber, quartered lengthwise and sliced
2 tomatoes cut into wedges
1/4 C green onions, sliced thin
1/2 C oil and vinegar salad dressing
1 (8 oz.) pkg. mozzarella cheese, shredded

Place the beans into a large salad bowl.
Add the cucumbers, tomatoes and onions and toss to combine well.
Pour the dressing over the top and stir until the ingredients are well coated.
Sprinkle the cheese over the top and toss to combine.

Makes 4 servings

Bow Tie Melon Salad

1 1/2 C bow tie pasta
2 C cantaloupe, chunked
1 C Swiss cheese, cubed
2 T fresh mint, finely snipped
1/3 C poppy seed dressing
2 C watercress

Cook the pasta as directed on the package.
Drain well, rinse with cold water and drain again.
Place the pasta into a salad bowl.
Add the cantaloupe and cheese and toss until well combined.
Fold in the mint.
Pour the dressing over the salad and toss to coat.
Stir in the watercress.

Makes 4 servings

Refreshing Cucumber Salad Bowls

3 large cucumbers
1 (6 oz) can tuna in water, drained well
2 hard boiled eggs, chopped
1/2 c celery, chopped fine
1 tbsp sweet onion, chopped fine
1/4 c mayonnaise
2 tbsp relish
1 tsp. lemon juice
1/4 tsp. pepper
1/2 c Cheddar cheese, shredded

Cut the cucumber in half longwise.
Remove the seeds and cut the bottom so the cucumbers set flat.
Place the tuna, eggs, celery and onion into a large mixing bowl.
Stir slightly to help breakup the tuna.
Add the mayonnaise and relish.
Stir together until the mayonnaise is slightly smooth.
Pour in the lemon juice.
Sprinkle in the pepper.
Stir to mix well.
Sprinkle in the cheese and continue stirring until all the ingredients are incorporated together.
Fill each cucumber half with the tuna mixture.

Cucumber boats can be filled with any type of salad. Egg salad, chicken salad, Greek salad or even ham salad.

Fruit Salad with Zest

1 C of blueberries
1 C of plums, sliced
1 C pitted cherries, sliced
1 C cantaloupe, chopped
1 C strawberries, sliced
1 C peaches, sliced
1 C of small green grapes
1 C of raspberries
1/4 C of lime juice
2 tbsp of honey
1 tsp grated lime peel
1 C lemon lime flavored sparkling water, chilled
Mint sprigs
In a 2 quart glass bowl layer the fruit in the order they are listed above.
Cover the bowl and chill 3 hours.
Just before serving place the lime juice into a small bowl.
Whisk in the honey and lime peel.
Add the sparkling water and stir until blended in well.
Pour the mixture over the layered fruit.
Garnish the top with the mint sprigs.

Makes 8 servings

Make Ahead Veggie Pasta Salad

2 C spiral pasta
1 zucchini, cubed
1/2 C ripe olives, sliced
1/2 C sweet red pepper, chopped
1/4 C onion, chopped
1/2 C of mayonnaise
1/4 C of sour cream
1 1/4 tsp dill
1/2 tsp salt
1/2 tsp ground mustard
1/4 tsp pepper
1/4 tsp garlic powder

Cook the pasta according to the directions on the package.
Drain the pasta well then rinse with cold water.
Place the pasta in a large serving bowl.
Gently stir in the zucchini, olives, red pepper and onion.
Place the mayonnaise and sour cream together in a mixing bowl.
Whisk in the dill, salt, mustard, pepper and garlic powder until blended together well.
Pour the mixture over the pasta salad.
Gently stir to coat.
Cover and chill at least 2 hour but preferably overnight.

Makes 8 servings

Steak Salad with Asian Chili Sauce

What You Need:
1 lb. beef flank stead
1 T soy sauce
8 oz. rice noodles
1 cucumber
1/2 C Asian sweet chili sauce
1/2 C of water
1 C fresh julienned carrot
Fresh cilantro

How to Make It:
Allow the broiler to preheat.
Brush the steak on both sides with the soy sauce.
Place he steak on the broiler pan rack.
Broil 5 inches from the heat for 18 minutes or until a meat thermometer reaches 160 degrees for medium done, turning once during cooking time.
Remove the steak to a platter and slice in thin strips across the grain.
Cook the rice noodles according to package directions.
Drain the noodles well and rinse under cool water.
Slice the cucumbers crosswise into three sections.
With a vegetable peeler cut ribbons lengthwise from each piece.
Place the chili sauce into a mixing bowl.
Whisk the water into the chili sauce until well combined.
Divide the steak, noodles, cucumber ribbons and carrots into four serving bowls.
Pour 1/4 of the sauce over each salad.
Sprinkle the cilantro over the top of each salad just before serving.

Makes 4 servings

Potato and Pea Salad

1 Tablespoon butter
1 Tablespoon flour
1/2 teaspoon salt
1 Cup milk
1 1/2 Cups new potatoes, cooked
1 pint fresh green peas, cooked and drained

Melt butter in pan, blend in flour and salt. Whisk together until well combined. Gradually add milk. Continue blending together. Cook until bubbly and thick. Add cooked potatoes and cooked peas. Serve warm.

Almond Cranberry Pasta Salad

1 (10 oz) pkg. plain couscous
1 C dried cranberries
3/4 C green onions, chopped
3/4 C sweet yellow pepper, chopped
3/4 C almonds, toasted
1/3 C lemon juice
1/4 C olive oil
1/2 t paprika
1/4 t salt
1/8 t pepper

Prepare the couscous as directed on the package.
When the couscous is cooked, place it in a large salad bowl and use a fork to fluff.
Cover the bowl and refrigerate 30 minutes or until chilled completely through.
When chilled remove the couscous from the refrigerator and stir in the cranberries.
Add the onions, sweet pepper and almonds and toss to combine all the ingredients.
Place the lemon juice into a small mixing bowl.
Add the oil, paprika, salt and pepper.
Use a whisk to mix the ingredients together well.
Drizzle the dressing into the salad and toss to coat.
Cover and refrigerate 1 hour before serving.

Sweet Red Apple Slaw

1 lg. head of cabbage, shredded
4 carrots, shredded
2 medium sweet red apples, chopped fine
1 C mayonnaise
1/4 C sugar
2 T white vinegar
1/2 t salt
1/4 t pepper

Place the cabbage in a large salad bowl.
Add the carrots and toss to combine.
Place the chopped apples in the bowl and toss again.
In a separate bowl, whisk together the mayonnaise, sugar and vinegar.
Sprinkle in the salt and pepper and whisk well to combine.
Pour the dressing into the cabbage mixture.
Toss with 2 forks to cover well.
Cover and refrigerate to chill through before serving.

Serving Size: 12

Made in the USA
Lexington, KY
23 February 2017